Book 1

C Programming Success in a Day

BY SAM KEY

&

Book 2
JavaScript Professional Programming Made Easy

BY SAM KEY

Book 1

C Programming Success in a Day

BY SAM KEY

Beginners' Guide To Fast, Easy And Efficient Learning Of C Programming

Programming #12:C Programming Success in a Day & JavaScript Professional Programming Made Easy

Programming #12:C Programming Success in a Day & JavaScript Professional Programming Made Easy

Table of Contents

Programming #12:C Programming Success in a Day & JavaScript Professional Programming Made Easy

Introduction

I want to thank you and congratulate you for purchasing the book, "C Programming Success in a Day – Beginners guide to fast, easy and efficient learning of Cc programming".

C. is one of the most popular and most used programming languages back then and today. Many expert developers have started with learning C in order to become knowledgeable in computer programming. In some grade schools and high schools, C programming is included on their curriculum.

If you are having doubts learning the language, do not. C is actually easy to learn. Compared to C++, C is much simpler and offer little. You do not need spend years to become a master of this language.

This book will tackle the basics when it comes to C. It will cover the basic functions you need in order to create programs that can produce output and accept input. Also, in the later chapters, you will learn how to make your program capable of simple thinking. And lastly, the last chapters will deal with teaching you how to create efficient programs with the help of loops.

Anyway, before you start programming using C, you need to get some things ready. First, you will need a compiler. A compiler is a program that will translate, compile, or convert your lines of code as an executable file. It means that, you will need a compiler for you to be able to run the program you have developed.

In case you are using this book as a supplementary source of information and you are taking a course of C, you might already have a compiler given to you by your instructor. If you are not, you can get one of the compilers that are available on the internet from MinGW.org.

You will also need a text editor. One of the best text editors you can use is Notepad++. It is free and can be downloadable from the internet. Also, it works well with MinGW's compiler.

Programming #12:C Programming Success in a Day & JavaScript Professional Programming Made Easy

In case you do not have time to configure or install those programs, you can go and get Microsoft's Visual C++ program. It contains all the things you need in order to practice developing programs using C or C++.

The content of this book was simplified in order for you to comprehend the ideas and practices in developing programs in C easily. Thanks again for purchasing this book. I hope you enjoy it!

Programming #12:C Programming Success in a Day & JavaScript Professional Programming Made Easy

Chapter 1: Hello World – the Basics

When coding a C program, you must start your code with the function 'main'. By the way, a function is a collection of action that aims to achieve one or more goals. For example, a vegetable peeler has one function, which is to remove a skin of a vegetable. The peeler is composed of parts (such as the blade and handle) that will aid you to perform its function. A C function is also composed of such components and they are the lines of codes within it.

Also, take note that in order to make your coding life easier, you will need to include some prebuilt headers or functions from your compiler.

To give you an idea on what C code looks like, check the sample below:

```
#include <stdio.h>

int main()

{

        printf( "Hello World!\n" );

        getchar();

        return 0;

}
```

As you can see in the first line, the code used the #include directive to include the stdio.h in the program. In this case, the stdio.h will provide you with access to functions such as printf and getchar.

Programming #12:C Programming Success in a Day & JavaScript Professional Programming Made Easy

Main Declaration

After that, the second line contains int main(). This line tells the compiler that there exist a function named main. The int in the line indicates that the function main will return an integer or number.

Curly Braces

The next line contains a curly brace. In C programming, curly braces indicate the start and end of a code block or a function. A code block is a series of codes joined together in a series. When a function is called by the program, all the line of codes inside it will be executed.

Printf()

The printf function, which follows the opening curly brace is the first line of code in your main function or code block. Like the function main, the printf also have a code block within it, which is already created and included since you included <stdio.h> in your program. The function of printf is to print text into your program's display window.

Beside printf is the value or text that you want to print. It should be enclosed in parentheses to abide standard practice. The value that the code want to print is Hello World!. To make sure that printf to recognize that you want to print a string and display the text properly, it should be enclosed inside double quotation marks.

By the way, in programming, a single character is called a character while a sequence of characters is called a string.

Escape Sequence

You might have noticed that the sentence is followed by a \n. In C, \n means new line. Since your program will have problems if you put a new line or press enter on the value of the printf, it is best to use its text equivalent or the escape sequence of the new line.

8

Programming #12:C Programming Success in a Day & JavaScript Professional Programming Made Easy

By the way, the most common escape sequences used in C are:

\t = tab

\f = new page

\r = carriage return

\b = backspace

\v = vertical tab

Semicolons

After the last parenthesis, a semicolon follows. And if you look closer, almost every line of code ends with it. The reasoning behind that is that the semicolon acts as an indicator that it is the end of the line of code or command. Without it, the compiler will think that the following lines are included in the printf function. And if that happens, you will get a syntax error.

Getchar()

Next is the getchar() function. Its purpose is to receive user input from the keyboard. Many programmers use it as a method on pausing a program and letting the program wait for the user to interact with it before it executes the next line of code. To make the program move through after the getchar() function, the user must press the enter key.

In the example, if you compile or run it without getchar(), the program will open the display or the console, display the text, and then immediately close. Without the break provided by the getchar() function, the computer will execute those commands instantaneously. And the program will open and close so fast that you will not be able to even see the Hello World text in the display.

Programming #12:C Programming Success in a Day & JavaScript Professional Programming Made Easy

Return Statement

The last line of code in the function is return 0. The return statement is essential in function blocks. When the program reaches this part, the return statement will tell the program its value. Returning the 0 value will make the program interpret that the function or code block that was executed successfully.

And at the last line of the example is the closing curly brace. It signifies that the program has reached the end of the function.

It was not that not hard, was it? With that example alone, you can create simple programs that can display text. Play around with it a bit and familiarize yourself with C's basic syntax.

Programming #12:C Programming Success in a Day & JavaScript Professional Programming Made Easy

Chapter 2: Basic Input Output

After experimenting with what you learned in the previous chapter, you might have realized that it was not enough. It was boring. And just displaying what you typed in your program is a bit useless.

This time, this chapter will teach you how to create a program that can interact with the user. Check this code example:

```
#include <stdio.h>

int main()

{

        int number_container;

        printf( "Enter any number you want! " );

        scanf( "%d", &number_container );

        printf( "The number you entered is %d", number_container );

        getchar();

        return 0;

}
```

Variables

You might have noticed the int number_container part in the first line of the code block. int number_container is an example of variable declaration. To declare a variable in C, you must indicate the variable type first, and then the name of the variable name.

In the example, int was indicated as the variable or data type, which means the variable is an integer. There are other variable types in C such as float for floating-point numbers, char for characters, etc. Alternatively, the name number_container was indicated as the variable's name or identifier.

Variables are used to hold values throughout the program and code blocks. The programmer can let them assign a value to it and retrieve its value when it is needed.

For example:

```
int number_container;
number_container = 3;
printf ( "The variables value is %d", number_container );
```

In that example, the first line declared that the program should create an integer variable named number_container. The second line assigned a value to the variable. And the third line makes the program print the text together with the value of the variable. When executed, the program will display:

The variables value is 3

You might have noticed the %d on the printf line on the example. The %d part indicates that the next value that will be printed will be an integer. Also, the quotation on the printf ended after %d. Why is that?

In order to print the value of a variable, it must be indicated with the double quotes. If you place double quotes on the variables name, the compiler will treat it as a literal string. If you do this:

Programming #12:C Programming Success in a Day & JavaScript Professional Programming Made Easy

```
int number_container;

number_container = 3;

printf ( "The variables value is number_container" );
```

The program will display:

The variables value is number_container

By the way, you can also use %i as a replacement for %d.

Assigning a value to a variable is simple. Just like in the previous example, just indicate the name of variable, follow it with an equal sign, and declare its value.

When creating variables, you must make sure that each variable will have unique names. Also, the variables should never have the same name as functions. In addition, you can declare multiple variables in one line by using commas. Below is an example:

```
int first_variable, second_variable, third_variable;
```

Those three variables will be int type variables. And again, never forget to place a semicolon after your declaration.

When assigning a value or retrieving the value of a variable, make sure that you declare its existence first. If not, the compiler will return an error since it will try to access something that does not exist yet.

13

Programming #12:C Programming Success in a Day & JavaScript Professional Programming Made Easy

Scanf()

In the first example in this chapter, you might have noticed the scanf function. The scanf function is also included in the <stdio.h>. Its purpose is to retrieve text user input from the user.

After the program displays the 'Enter any number you want' text, it will proceed in retrieving a number from the user. The cursor will be appear after the text since the new line escape character was no included in the printf.

The cursor will just blink and wait for the user to enter any characters or numbers. To let the program get the number the user typed and let it proceed to the next line of code, he must press the Enter key. Once he does that, the program will display the text 'The number you entered is' and the value of the number the user inputted a while ago.

To make the scanf function work, you must indicate the data type it needs to receive and the location of the variable where the value that scanf will get will be stored. In the example:

```
scanf( "%d", &number_container );
```

The first part "%d" indicates that the scanf function must retrieve an integer. On the other hand, the next part indicates the location of the variable. You must have noticed the ampersand placed in front of the variable's name. The ampersand retrieves the location of the variable and tells it to the function.

Unlike the typical variable value assignment, scanf needs the location of the variable instead of its name alone. Due to that, without the ampersand, the function will not work.

Programming #12:C Programming Success in a Day & JavaScript Professional Programming Made Easy

Math or Arithmetic Operators

Aside from simply giving number variables with values by typing a number, you can assign values by using math operators. In C, you can add, subtract, multiply, and divide numbers and assign the result to variables directly. For example:

int sum;

sum = 1 + 2;

If you print the value of sum, it will return a 3, which is the result of the addition of 1 and 2. By the way, the + sign is for addition, - for subtraction, * for multiplication, and / for division.

With the things you have learned as of now, you can create a simple calculator program. Below is an example code:

```
#include <stdio.h>
int main()
{
        int first_addend, second_addend, sum;
        printf( "Enter the first addend! " );
        scanf( "%d", &first_addend );
        printf( "\nEnter the second addend! " );
        scanf( "%d", &second_addend );
        sum = first_addend + second_addend;
        printf( "The sum of the two numbers is %d", sum );
```

```
getchar();

return 0;

}
```

Programming #12:C Programming Success in a Day & JavaScript Professional Programming Made Easy

Chapter 3: Conditional Statements

The calculator program seems nice, is it not? However, the previous example limits you on creating programs that only uses one operation, which is a bit disappointing. Well, in this chapter, you can improve that program with the help of if or conditional statements. And of course, learning this will improve your overall programming skills. This is the part where you will be able to make your program 'think'.

'If' statements can allow you to create branches in your code blocks. Using them allows you to let the program think and perform specific functions or actions depending on certain variables and situations. Below is an example:

```c
#include <stdio.h>

int main()

{

        int some_number;

        printf( "Welcome to Guess the Magic Number program. \n" );

        printf( "Guess the magic number to win. \n" );

        printf( "Type the magic number and press Enter: " );

        scanf( "%d", &some_number );

        if ( some_number == 3 ) {

                printf( "You guessed the right number! " );

        }

        getchar();

        return 0;
```

```
}
```

In the example, the if statement checked if the value of the variable some_number is equal to number 3. In case the user entered the number 3 on the program, the comparison between the variable some_number and three will return TRUE since the value of some_number 3 is true. Since the value that the if statement received was TRUE, then it will process the code block below it. And the result will be:

You guessed the right number!

If the user input a number other than three, the comparison will return a FALSE value. If that happens, the program will skip the code block in the if statement and proceed to the next line of code after the if statement's code block.

By the way, remember that you need to use the curly braces to enclosed the functions that you want to happen in case your if statement returns TRUE. Also, when inserting if statement, you do not need to place a semicolon after the if statement or its code block's closing curly brace. However, you will still need to place semicolons on the functions inside the code blocks of your if statements.

TRUE and FALSE

The if statement will always return TRUE if the condition is satisfied. For example, the condition in the if statement is 10 > 2. Since 10 is greater than 2, then it is true. On the other hand, the if statement will always return FALSE if the condition is not satisfied. For example, the condition in the if statement is 5 < 5. Since 5 is not less than 5, then the statement will return a FALSE.

Note that if statements only return two results: TRUE and FALSE. In computer programming, the number equivalent to TRUE is any nonzero number. In some cases, it is only the number 1. On the other hand, the number equivalent of FALSE is zero.

Operators

Also, if statements use comparison, Boolean, or relational and logical operators. Some of those operators are:

== – equal to

!= – not equal to

> – greater than

< – less than

>= – greater than or equal to

<= – less than or equal to

Else Statement

There will be times that you would want your program to do something else in case your if statement return FALSE. And that is what the else statement is for. Check the example below:

```
#include <stdio.h>
int main()
{
        int some_number;
        printf( "Welcome to Guess the Magic Number program. \n" );
        printf( "Guess the magic number to win. \n" );
```

```
printf( "Type the magic number and press Enter: " );

scanf( "%d", &some_number );

if ( some_number == 3 ) {

        printf( "You guessed the right number! " );

}

else {

        printf( "Sorry. That is the wrong number" );

}

getchar();

return 0;

}
```

If ever the if statement returns FALSE, the program will skip next to the else statement immediately. And since the if statement returns FALSE, it will immediately process the code block inside the else statement.

For example, if the number the user inputted on the program is 2, the if statement will return a FALSE. Due to that, the else statement will be processed, and the program will display:

Sorry. That is the wrong number

On the other hand, if the if statement returns TRUE, it will process the if statement's code block, but it will bypass all the succeeding else statements below it.

Programming #12:C Programming Success in a Day & JavaScript Professional Programming Made Easy

Else If

If you want more conditional checks on your program, you will need to take advantage of else if. Else if is a combination of the if and else statement. It will act like an else statement, but instead of letting the program execute the code block below it, it will perform another check as if it was an if statement. Below is an example:

```c
#include <stdio.h>

int main()

{
        int some_number;

        printf( "Welcome to Guess the Magic Number program. \n" );

        printf( "Guess the magic number to win. \n" );

        printf( "Type the magic number and press Enter: " );

        scanf( "%d", &some_number );

        if ( some_number == 3 ) {

                printf( "You guessed the right number! " );

        }

        else if ( some_number > 3 ){

                printf( "Your guess is too high!" );

        }

        else {

                printf( "Your guess is too low!" );

        }
```

```
        getchar();

        return 0;

}
```

In case the if statement returns FALSE, the program will evaluate the else if statement. If it returns TRUE, it will execute its code block and ignore the following else statements. However, if it is FALSE, it will proceed on the last else statement, and execute its code block. And just like before, if the first if statement returns true, it will disregard the following else and else if statements.

In the example, if the user inputs 3, he will get the You guessed the right number message. If the user inputs 4 or higher, he will get the Your guess is too high message. And if he inputs any other number, he will get a Your guess is too low message since any number aside from 3 and 4 or higher is automatically lower than 3.

With the knowledge you have now, you can upgrade the example calculator program to handle different operations. Look at the example and study it:

```
#include <stdio.h>

int main()

{

        int first_number, second_number, result, operation;

        printf( "Enter the first number: " );

        scanf( "%d", &first_number );

        printf( "\nEnter the second number: " );
```

```c
scanf( "%d", &second_number );
printf ( "What operation would you like to use? \n" );
printf ( "Enter 1 for addition. \n" );
printf ( "Enter 2 for subtraction. \n" );
printf ( "Enter 3 for multiplication. \n" );
printf ( "Enter 4 for division. \n" );
scanf( "%d", &operation );
if ( operation == 1 ) {
        result = first_number + second_number;
        printf( "The sum is %d", result );
}
else if ( operation == 2 ){
        result = first_number - second_number;
        printf( "The difference is %d", result );
}
else if ( operation == 3 ){
        result = first_number * second_number;
        printf( "The product is %d", result );
}
else if ( operation == 4 ){
        result = first_number / second_number;
        printf( "The quotient is %d", result );
}
```

```c
    else {

        printf( "You have entered an invalid choice." );

    }

    getchar();

    return 0;

}
```

Programming #12:C Programming Success in a Day & JavaScript Professional Programming Made Easy

Chapter 4: Looping in C

The calculator's code is getting better, right? As of now, it is possible that you are thinking about the programs that you could create with the usage of the conditional statements.

However, as you might have noticed in the calculator program, it seems kind of painstaking to use. You get to only choose one operation every time you run the program. When the calculation ends, the program closes. And that can be very annoying and unproductive.

To solve that, you must create loops in the program. Loops are designed to let the program execute some of the functions inside its code blocks. It effectively eliminates the need to write some same line of codes. It saves the time of the programmer and it makes the program run more efficiently.

There are four different ways in creating a loop in C. In this chapter, two of the only used and simplest loop method will be discussed. To grasp the concept of looping faster, check the example below:

```c
#include <stdio.h>

int main()
{
        int some_number;

        int guess_result;

        guess_result = 0;


        printf( "Welcome to Guess the Magic Number program. \n" );

        printf( "Guess the magic number to win. \n" );
```

```c
printf( "You have unlimited chances to guess the number. \n" );


while ( guess_result == 0 ) {


        printf( "Guess the magic number: " );
        scanf( "%d", &some_number );
        if ( some_number == 3 ) {
                printf( "You guessed the right number! \n" );
                guess_result = 1;
        }
        else if ( some_number > 3 ){
                printf( "Your guess is too high! \n" );
                guess_result = 0;
        }
        else {
                printf( "Your guess is too low! \n" );
                guess_result = 0;
        }
}
printf( "Thank you for playing. Press Enter to exit this program." );
getchar();
return 0;

}
```

Programming #12:C Programming Success in a Day & JavaScript Professional Programming Made Easy

While Loop

In this example, the while loop function was used. The while loop allows the program to execute the code block inside it as long as the condition is met or the argument in it returns TRUE. It is one of the simplest loop function in C. In the example, the condition that the while loop requires is that the guess_result variable should be equal to 0.

As you can see, in order to make sure that the while loop will start, the value of the guess_result variable was set to 0.

If you have not noticed it yet, you can actually nest code blocks within code blocks. In this case, the code block of the if and else statements were inside the code block of the while statement.

Anyway, every time the code reaches the end of the while statement and the guess_result variable is set to 0, it will repeat itself. And to make sure that the program or user experience getting stuck into an infinite loop, a safety measure was included.

In the example, the only way to escape the loop is to guess the magic number. If the if statement within the while code block was satisfied, its code block will run. In that code block, a line of code sets the variable guess_result's value to 1. This effectively prevent the while loop from running once more since the guess_result's value is not 0 anymore, which makes the statement return a FALSE.

Once that happens, the code block of the while loop and the code blocks inside it will be ignored. It will skip to the last printf line, which will display the end program message 'Thank you for playing. Press Enter to exit this program'.

Programming #12:C Programming Success in a Day & JavaScript Professional Programming Made Easy

For Loop

The for loop is one of the most handy looping function in C. And its main use is to perform repetitive commands on a set number of times. Below is an example of its use:

```c
#include <stdio.h>

int main()

{

    int some_number;

    int x;

    int y;


    printf( "Welcome to Guess the Magic Number program. \n" );

    printf( "Guess the magic number to win. \n" );

    printf( "You have only three chance of guessing. \n" );

    printf( "If you do not get the correct answer after guessing three times. \n" );

    printf( "This program will be terminated. \n" );


    for (x = 0; x < 3; x++) {

        y = 3 - x;

        printf( "The number of guesses that you have left is: %d", y );

        printf( "\nGuess the magic number: " );

        scanf( "%d", &some_number );
```

28

```c
        if ( some_number == 3 ) {

                printf( "You guessed the right number! \n" );

                x = 4;

        }

        else if ( some_number > 3 ){

                printf( "Your guess is too high! \n " );

        }

        else {

                printf( "Your guess is too low! \n " );

        }

    }

    printf( "Press the Enter button to close this program. \n" );

    getchar();

    getchar();

    return 0;

}
```

The for statement's argument section or part requires three things. First, the initial value of the variable that will be used. In this case, the example declared that x = 0. Second, the condition. In the example, the for loop will run until x has a value lower than 3. Third, the variable update line. Every time the for loop loops, the variable update will be executed. In this case, the variable update that will be triggered is x++.

Programming #12:C Programming Success in a Day & JavaScript Professional Programming Made Easy

Increment and Decrement Operators

By the way, x++ is a variable assignment line. The x is the variable and the ++ is an increment operator. The function of an increment operator is to add 1 to the variable where it was placed. In this case, every time the program reads x++, the program will add 1 to the variable x. If x has a value of 10, the increment operator will change variable x's value to 11.

On the other hand, you can also use the decrement operator instead of the increment operator. The decrement operator is done by place -- next to a variable. Unlike the increment operator, the decrement subtracts 1 to its operand.

Just like the while loop, the for loop will run as long as its condition returns TRUE. However, the for loop has a built in safety measure and variable declaration. You do not need to declare the value needed for its condition outside the statement. And the safety measure to prevent infinite loop is the variable update. However, it does not mean that it will be automatically immune to infinite loops. Poor programming can lead to it. For example:

```
for (x = 1; x > 1; x++) {

        /* Insert Code Block Here */

}
```

In this example, the for loop will enter into an infinite loop unless a proper means of escape from the loop is coded inside its code block.

The structure of the for loop example is almost the same with while loop. The only difference is that the program is set to loop for only three times. In this case, it only allows the user to guess three times or until the value of variable x does not reach 3 or higher.

Every time the user guesses wrong, the value of x is incremented, which puts the loop closer in ending. However, in case the user guesses right, the code block of the if statement assigns a value higher than 3 to variable x in order to escape the loop and end the program.

Conclusion

Thank you again for purchasing this book!

I hope this book was able to help you to learn the basics of C programming. The next step is to learn the other looping methods, pointers, arrays, strings, command line arguments, recursion, and binary trees.

Finally, if you enjoyed this book, please take the time to share your thoughts and post a review on Amazon. We do our best to reach out to readers and provide the best value we can. Your positive review will help us achieve that. It'd be greatly appreciated!
Thank you and good luck!

Book 2

JavaScript Professional Programming Made Easy

BY SAM KEY

Expert JavaScripts Programming Language Success in a Day for Any Computer User!

Programming #12:C Programming Success in a Day & JavaScript Professional Programming Made Easy

Table Of Contents

Programming #12:C Programming Success in a Day & JavaScript Professional Programming Made Easy

Programming #12:C Programming Success in a Day & JavaScript Professional Programming Made Easy

Introduction

I want to thank you and congratulate you for purchasing the book, "Professional JavaScript Programming Made Easy: Expert JavaScripts Programming Language Success In A Day for Any Computer User!"

This book contains proven steps and strategies on how to code JavaScript from scratch.

This book will give you a solid idea on how JavaScript works and how it can be applied to your web pages. This is an ideal book that every beginner should read. However, it is required that you already know HTML and CSS.

Familiarity with other programming languages such as Java, Visual Basic, and C is a plus since it will make it easier for you to learn and understand the concepts behind the processes involved in coding JavaScript.

Every explanation in the book will be accompanied by an example. Those examples will be shown in Courier New font; in case that font is not available, it will be shown in a monospaced generic family font instead.

To learn and code JavaScript, all you need is a text editing tool such as Notepad in Windows or TextEdit in Macintosh computers. However, it is recommend that you use a source code editor or a text editing tool with syntax highlighting that supports HTML, CSS, and JavaScript languages to speed up your learning and reduce the typos you will make.

One of the best and free source code editor tools you can get from the internet is Notepad++. It will be discussed in the last chapter of the book.

Thanks again for purchasing this book, I hope you enjoy it!

Programming #12:C Programming Success in a Day & JavaScript Professional Programming Made Easy

Chapter 1: Introduction to JavaScript

JavaScript is a scripting or programming language that is mainly used for web pages. Almost all websites use it to provide their visitors a richer browsing experience. Compared to coding HTML, JavaScript is real programming.

It is safe to say that JavaScript is the most popular and most widely used programming language in the world. JavaScript is easy to learn, and that is why web developers or even hobbyists can use it after a few days of studying it.

Unlike other programming languages, JavaScript is easy to learn and apply practically. The programs or scripts created from JavaScript are used by millions of people – even though they do not know they are already using them.

JavaScript can turn your old HTML files, which are static, into dynamic. You can embed JavaScript into your files for you to deliver web pages with dynamic content and appearance.

To embed JavaScript to your HTML file, you must enclose your script inside script HTML tags (<script></script>). Commonly, you should place the script tags inside the head HTML tags (<head></head>). However, there will be times that you might want or need to place them inside your page's body (<body></body>).

On the other hand, JavaScript can be placed in an external file and linked on a web page to work. It will be considered to be a part of the HTML file being parsed by the browser once it is linked.

Client and Server Side Scripting

In web development, JavaScript is termed as a client side scripting language. All the scripts that you write in JavaScript are executed on the client side, which is your or your visitors' browser.

On the other hand, PHP and ASP are server side scripting languages. As you might have guessed, the scripts or programs created using those two are executed on the server and their results are usually sent to the client.

The two complete the concept of DHTML (Dynamic HTML). When you use client and server side scripting, your pages will become more dynamic and interactive. With them, you can create social media websites, online games, and even your own search engine. And those statements are not exaggerated. You are truly a few steps away from greatness once you master JavaScript and a server side scripting language.

However, take note that learning client side scripting is a prerequisite before learning server side scripting. After all, most of the functions and features that you will create using server side scripting will require or need the support of client side scripting. Also, client side scripting is a good introduction to programming for web developers who have no experience or even any idea on how programming works.

Before you start learning and applying JavaScript to your web documents, you should learn and master HTML and CSS. In JavaScript, you will be mostly dealing with HTML elements, so it is a requirement that you know about HTML elements and attributes.

Programming #12:C Programming Success in a Day & JavaScript Professional Programming Made Easy

Alternatively, if you want to use JavaScript to perform advanced styling on your document such as animations and dynamic layouts, then you should have a solid background on CSS.

To give you a short summary of the relationship between HTML, CSS, and JavaScript, take note of these pointers:

- HTML is used to define the content and elements of your web page.

- CSS is used to specify or precisely define the appearance and layout of your web page.

- JavaScript is used to create functionalities in your web page. It can also be used to define content like HTML and define appearances like CSS.

With JavaScript, you can fully control everything on your web page. You can change an HTML element's content. For example, you can change the text content of a paragraph element with JavaScript.

You can also change the value of one of the attributes of an HTML element. For example, you can change the HREF attribute of a link you inserted on your document.

And lastly, you can change the CSS or styling values of an HTML element. For example, you can change the font-weight of one of your headers in your web document with JavaScript, too.

Also, with JavaScript, you have full control on when it will be applied, unlike CSS. You can run your scripts before the page loads, while the page is loading, after the page loaded, and while your user browses the page.

On the other hand, you can make those changes automatic or triggered by the visitor. You can add other factors such as time of the day, specific user actions, or user browsing behavior to trigger those changes or functions.

Programming #12:C Programming Success in a Day & JavaScript Professional Programming Made Easy

Chapter 2: HTML DOM and Assigning Values

How can JavaScript do all of that? It can do all of that because it takes advantage of the HTML DOM or Document Object Model. JavaScript can access, modify, and remove any HTML element together with its properties by using HTML DOM.

Assigning Attribute Values with JavaScript

With CSS, you have dealt with selectors. By using the right selector, you can change the CSS style of a specific element, group or class of elements, group of similar elements, handpicked elements, or all of the elements in your page. By this point, you must already know how id's and classes works.

JavaScript almost works like that, too. To change the content of an element, value of an element's property or attribute, or style of an element, you will need to select them first and assign a value. Below is an example of using JavaScript to change a paragraph element's (which has a value of "testparagraph" for its id attribute) font size:

```
<head>
<script>
document.getElementById("testparagraph" ).style.fontSize = "17px";
</script>
</head>
<body>
<p id='testparagraph' >This a paragraph. This is another sentence. This is the last sentence.</p>
</body>
```

The previous line's equivalent to CSS is:

```
#testparagraph {font-size: 17px;}
```

They have different syntax, but they will have the same result. In the CSS example, the paragraph with the "testparagraph" id was selected by placing a pound sign and typing the id value.

In JavaScript, "testparagraph" was selected using DOM. If you will translate the example JavaScript line to plain English, the line says to the browser that the line of code pertains to something or will do something within the document, which is your webpage.

Then the next part tells the browser that you are looking for a certain element that has a value of "testparagraph" on its id attribute. The next part tells the browser that you will do something to the style attribute of the "testparagraph" element. And the last part tells the browser that you will assign a value on the fontSize within the element's style attribute.

In JavaScript, the equals sign (=) means that you will assign a value to the variable or property on its left. And the value that you will assign on the variable or property is on the right.

On the example, you will assign the value "17px" to the fontSize style attribute of the element "testparagraph" that is located within your HTML document. The

38

semicolon at the end tells the browser that it is the end of the line for that code, and it should parse the next line for it to execute.

Browser Parsing Behavior

By default, that previous JavaScript example will not work. The reason is that browsers read and execute HTML documents line by line – from the starting tag of the html tag, the browser will perform scripts, apply CSS values, place the HTML elements, place their specific contents, etcetera, until the browser reach the closing html tag.

In the example, the line asks the browser for an element that has the value "testparagraph" in its id attribute in the document. Unfortunately, the browser has not reached the body of the document where the definition of the element "testparagraph" resides.

Because of that, the browser will return an error saying that there is no element that has that attribute. You cannot assign a value for the attribute font size style to a nonexistent or null object. Hence, when the browser reaches the definition of the element "testparagraph", its font size will not be changed to the value you have set in the JavaScript code.

The solution to that is simple: you can place the script after the part where the element "testparagraph" was defined, and that is any location after the closing paragraph of the element "testparagraph".

Chapter 3: JavaScript Statements

In the last part of the previous chapter, the book loosely discussed about how browsers read HTML files and JavaScript lines and how you can assign values to an attribute. This chapter will supplement you with further discussions about that and JavaScript statements.

To construct a program using a programming language, you will need to write lines of codes. Those lines of codes are called statements. A statement is a line of code that contains an instruction for the computer to execute. In JavaScript, the one that executes the code is your internet browser.

Statements in JavaScript might contain the following: Keywords, Expressions, Operators, Comments, and Values. Below are sample lines of JavaScript that this chapter will dissect; this is done so that you will know the parts that comprise JavaScript statements:

var x; // This is a comment line.

var y; // To create one, you must place two forward slashes.

var z; // Comment lines are ignored by the browser.

x = 1 + 1; // So you can place them before or after a statement.

y = "Hello World." // And it will not affect the syntax.

z = 10 // But do not put them in the middle of a statement.

Keywords

In the example, the word var is a keyword. Typically, keywords are reserved words that you cannot use in your program except when you need to use their purpose. In the sample statements, the keyword var tells the browser to create a variable named x. Variables will be discussed later.

Expressions

On the other hand, 1 + 1 is an expression and the + and = sign are examples of operators. Expressions, in computer programming, are combinations of operators, values, constants, and variables that will be interpreted by the computer to produce a result. In x = 1 + 1, the browser will compute or evaluate that expression and return a value of 2. Expressions are not limited to arithmetic operations in JavaScript. Expressions can be in form of Boolean comparison, string operations, and etcetera.

Values

There are two values types that you will see and use in JavaScript. The first type is fixed or literal values; the second type is variables.

Literal Values

Numbers, Strings (text enclosed in single or double quotes), and even Expressions are literal values. In the example, the parts "Hello World" (string), 10 (number), and 1 + 1 (expression) are literal values.

Variables

On the other hand, variables are data containers. Variables can contain literal values such as strings, numbers, arrays, expressions, and even objects.

Programming #12:C Programming Success in a Day & JavaScript Professional Programming Made Easy

To use or create one, you must name it or create an identifier for it. Identifiers are combinations of letters, underscores, and dollar signs and must not be the same with any keywords or reserved words in JavaScript.

However, take note that identifiers must start with a letter, an underscore, or a dollar sign only. Starting with a number will return an error, and including symbols other than underscores and dollar signs will not be accepted by JavaScript.

Local Variable and Global Variables

There are two types of variables in JavaScript. The first one is local and the second one is global. The type of variable depends on where it was declared. The difference between them is how they are handled in the script.

Variables that are declared outside of functions will become a global variable. And variables that are declared inside functions will become a local variable.

Global variables will stay on the memory until the web page is closed. It can be referenced and used anywhere in the script. On the other hand, local variables will only stay on the memory until the browser finishes executing the function where the variable was declared. It can be only referenced and used by the function where it was declared. Functions will be discussed later in this book.

In the sample JavaScript statements, the letters x, y, and z are global variables.

To create a variable in JavaScript, you must use the var keyword – just like in the previous example. To assign values to them, you can use the equal operator.

Operators

There are multiple of operators that you can use in JavaScript. And it can be categorized into the following:

- Arithmetic

- Assignment

- String

- Comparison

- Logical

- Conditional

- Bitwise

- Typeof

- Delete Unary +

Only the first four types of operators are mostly the ones that you will frequently use during your early days of JavaScript programming: Arithmetic, Assignment,

String, and Comparison. The remaining operators are typically used for advanced projects and might be confusing for beginners.

On the other hand, take note that some of the operator symbols may serve two purposes or more. For example, the + sign can be used as an arithmetic, string, or unary + operator depending on the condition or your goal.

Comments

You might already have an idea on what comments are. As mentioned before, they are ignored by browsers, and their only function is to serve as reminders or notes for you – just like the comments in HTML. You can create a new line of comment by using two forward slashes. If you want to create a block of comment, start it with /* and end it with */.

Programming #12:C Programming Success in a Day & JavaScript Professional Programming Made Easy

Chapter 4: JavaScript's Basic Syntax

For the browser to execute a JavaScript statement, the statement must follow the correct syntax and must only have one instruction (this may vary depending the code).

Just a small mistake in the syntax will make the computer do something different from what you want to happen or it might not do nothing and return an error.

If you have a large block of code and one of the statements gets an error, the browser will not execute the lines that follow the statement that generated an error.

Due to that, it is important that you always check your code and avoid creating mistakes to make sure that you will achieve the things you want to happen with JavaScript.

JavaScript Syntax

JavaScript, just like other computer languages, follow syntax. In computer programming, syntax is a set of rules that you must follow when writing codes.

One of the syntax rules in JavaScript is to terminate each statement with a colon. It is like placing a dot in every sentence you make.

This rule is flexible due to ASI (Automatic Semicolon Inserting). Even if you do not place a semicolon at the end of your statement, once you start a new line, the previous line will be considered as a complete statement – as if it has a semicolon at the end. However, not placing semicolons is bad practice since it might produce bugs and errors.

Another rule is to make sure that you close brackets, parentheses, and quotations in your code. For example, leaving a dangling curly brace will result in an error. And with quotation marks, if you started with a single quote, end it with a single quote. If you start with a double quote, end with a double quote.

Take note that JavaScript is a case-sensitive language. Unlike HTML wherein you can use lower, upper, and mixed case on tags and attributes, JavaScript will return an error once you use the wrong case for a method or variable. For example, changing the capitalization of the letter b in the getElementById will result to an error.

Never create variables that have the similar name with keywords or reserved words. Also, always declare variables. If you do not explicitly declare them and use them on your statements, you might get unexpected results or a reference error. For example:

var y;

var z;

y = 1;

z = 1 + x;

Once your browser reads the last line, no value will be assigned to z because the browser will return a reference error.

That is just a few of the rules in JavaScript's syntax. Some methods and keywords follow certain syntax. Remember them to prevent yourself from the hassle of unneeded debugging.

Chapter 5: Functions and Events

You already know by now what statements are and how to write statements in accordance to JavaScript's syntax rules. You also know how to assign values to an HTML element's attribute by using JavaScript. In this chapter, you will know how to create functions or methods.

A function is a block of statements that you can call or invoke anytime to execute. In other programming languages, functions are called subroutines, methods, or procedures. The statements inside a function will not be immediately executed when the browser parses the HTML document. It will only run or be executed if it is called or invoked.

Purposes of Functions

What are the purposes of functions? First, it allows you to control when to execute a block of statements as explained previously.

Second, it allows you to create 'mini' programs in your script. For example, if you want to make a paragraph to be centered align, to have a heavier font, and to have a bigger font size when you click the paragraph, you can create a function for that goal and capture an event that will trigger that function once you click on the paragraph.

Third, creating functions is a good way to separate lengthy blocks of statements into smaller chunks. Maintaining and debugging your script will be much easier with functions.

Fourth, it can effectively lessen redundancy in your script. Instead of writing the same sequence of statements repeatedly in your script, you can just create a function, and just call it again when you need the browser to execute the statements within it once more.

Creating Functions

To create a function, you will need to use the keyword function. When you create a function you must follow a simple syntax. Below is an example of a function:

function MakeBolderAndBigger(elementID) {
document.getElementById(elementID).style.fontSize = "20px";
document.getElementById(elementID).style.fontWeight = "20px";
}

In the example, the keyword function was followed with MakeBolderAndBigger. That part is the function's name. Naming a function has the same rules with naming a variable identifier.

After the function's name, there is elementID which is enclosed in parentheses. That part of the function is called a parameter. You can place as many parameters that you want or none at all. If you place multiple parameters, you must separate them with a comma and a space. If you are not going to use parameters, just leave it blank but never forget to place the parentheses.

A parameter stores that value or the function arguments that was placed on it when the function is invoked. That parameter will act as local variable in the function. This part will be discussed further later.

Programming #12:C Programming Success in a Day & JavaScript Professional Programming Made Easy

Then, after the parameter, you will see a curly brace. And after the statements, there is another curly brace.

The first brace act as a sign that tells the browsers that any statements following it is a code block for the function. The second brace tells the browsers that the code block is finished, and any line of code after it is not related to the function. Those are the rules you need to follow when creating a function.

Invoking Functions

There are two common ways to invoke a function. First, you can invoke it within your script. Second, you can invoke it by placing and triggering event handlers.

Invoke within Code

The first method of invoking functions is easy. All you need to do is to type the name of the function, and fill in the arguments that the function's parameters require. To invoke the example function using the first method, you can simply type this:

MakeBolderAndBigger("testparagraph");

Once your browser reads that, it will process the function. Since you have placed "testparagraph" as the argument for the parameter elementID, elementID will have a value of "testparagraph". It will now act as a variable.

When the browser executes the first statement in the function, which is document.getElementById(elementID).style.fontSize = "20px";, it will select the element "testparagraph" and change its font size value to 20px.

On the other hand, you can actually provide no argument for function parameters. If you do this instead:

MakeBolderAndBigger();

The browser will execute the function. However, since you did not store any value to the parameter, the parameter elementID will be undefined and will have the value undefined.

Because of that, when the first statement tries to look for the element with the id attribute of elementID, which has the value of undefined, it will return an error.

Once the browser finishes executing the function, it will return on reading the next line of code after the function invocation. For example:

MakeBolderAndBigger("testparagraph");
document.getElementById("testparagraph").style.color = "blue";

After the browser finishes executing the function MakeBolderAndBigger, it will proceed on executing the next statement below and make the font color of "testparagraph" to blue. The example above is the same as coding:

document.getElementById("testparagraph").style.fontSize = "20px";
document.getElementById("testparagraph").style.fontWeight = "20px";
document.getElementById("testparagraph").style.color = "blue";

Invoke with Events

Every action that a user does in a web page and every action that the browser performs are considered events. A few of those events are:

- When the page finishes loading

- When a user or script changes the content of a text field

45

Programming #12:C Programming Success in a Day & JavaScript Professional Programming Made Easy

- When a user click a button or an HTML element

- When a user presses on a keyboard key

To invoke a function when an event happens, you must tell the browser by placing some piece of codes in your page's HTML. Below is an example:
<button   onClick='MakeBolderAndBigger("testparagraph");'   >Invoke Function</button>
When a user clicks on that button element, it will trigger the function MakeBolderAndBigger. The syntax for that is simple. Just insert the event inside the opening tag of an HTML element that has the event that you want to capture, place an equal sign, place the function that you want to execute together with the arguments you need to place on it, and then enclose the function in quotes.

By the way, be wary of quotes. If you used a single quote to enclose the function, then use double quotes to enclose the values on your arguments. Just think of it as if you are assigning values on an element's style attribute in HTML. Also, as best practice, never forget to place a semicolon at the end.

As a reference, below are some of the events that you can use in HTML and JavaScript:

- onClick – triggers when the user clicks on the HTML element

- onMouseOver – triggers when the user hovers on the HTML element

- onMouseOut – triggers when the user's mouse pointers move out from the element's display

- onKeyDown – triggers when the user presses a keyboard key

- onChange – triggers when the user changes the content of a text field

- onLoad – triggers when the browser is done loading the body, images, frames, and other scripts

Programming #12:C Programming Success in a Day & JavaScript Professional Programming Made Easy

Chapter 6: Debugging, Text Editing Tool, and References

In modern browsers, most of JavaScript errors are handled automatically and ignored to prevent browsing disruption. So when testing your scripts when opening your HTML files on a browser, it is difficult to spot errors and debug.

Web Developer Consoles on Browsers

Fortunately, a few of those browsers have built-in developer consoles where you can monitor errors and the resources that your page generates and uses. One of those browsers that have this functionality is Google Chrome. To access its developer console, you can press F12 on your keyboard while a page is open on it. Pressing the key will open the developer tools panel within Chrome, and you can click on the Console tab to monitor the errors that your page generates. Aside from monitoring errors, you can use it to test statements, check the values of your variables, call functions, etc.

Text Editing Tool with Syntax Highlighting

You can get away with a few problems when writing HTML and CSS on typical text editing tools like Notepad. However, with JavaScript coding, using those ordinary tools is a challenge. Unlike the two, JavaScript has a strict and vast syntax. Just one typo in your script and you will start hunting bugs after you test the statements you wrote. After all, it is a programming language unlike HTML which is a markup language.

To make your life easier, it is best that you use a text editing tool with syntax highlighting when coding JavaScript. One of the best tools out there on the Web is Notepad++. It is free and it is as lightweight (in terms of resource usage) and as simple as Notepad.

The syntax highlighting will help you spot missing brackets and quotation marks. It will also prevent you from using keywords as variables since keywords are automatically highlighted in a different color, which will help you realize sooner that they are identifiers you cannot use for variables.

References

As of now, you have only learned the basics of how to code JavaScript. You might have been itching to change the values of other attributes in your HTML code, but you do not know the HTML DOM to use. On the other hand, you might be interested on knowing the other operators that you can use in your script.

The book has omitted most of them since it focused more on the coding process in JavaScript. Thankfully, you can just look up those values and operators on the net. To give you a head start, this a link to the JavaScript reference list made by the developers in the Mozilla Foundation: https://developer.mozilla.org/en-US/docs/Web/JavaScript/Reference.

Programming #12:C Programming Success in a Day & JavaScript Professional Programming Made Easy

Conclusion

Thank you again for purchasing this book!

I hope this book was able to help you to learn the basics of coding with JavaScript.

The next step is to:

Master the HTML DOM.

Become familiar with other keywords and their usage.

Finally, if you enjoyed this book, please take the time to share your thoughts and post a review on Amazon. We do our best to reach out to readers and provide the best value we can. Your positive review will help us achieve that. It'd be greatly appreciated!

Thank you and good luck!

Programming #12:C Programming Success in a Day & JavaScript Professional Programming Made Easy

Check Out My Other Books

Below you'll find some of my other popular books that are popular on Amazon and Kindle as well. Simply click on the links below to check them out. Alternatively, you can visit my author page on Amazon to see other work done by me.

Click here to check out C Programming Success in a Day on Amazon.

Click here to check out Android Programming in a Day on Amazon.

Click here to check out C ++ Programming Success in a Day on Amazon

Click here to check out C Programming Professional Made Easy on Amazon.

Click here to check out Python Programming in a Day on Amazon.

Click here to check out PHP Programming Professional Made Easy on Amazon.

Click here to check out HTML Professional Programming Made Easy on Amazon

Click here to check out CSS Programming Professional Made Easy on Amazon.

Click here to check out Windows 8 Tips for Beginners on Amazon.

Click here to check out the rest of Android Programming in a Day on Amazon.

Click here to check out the rest of Python Programming in a Day on Amazon.

Click here to check out JavaScript Programming Made Easy on Amazon

If the links do not work, for whatever reason, you can simply search for these titles on the Amazon website to find them.